To : Mike

From : Terry S.

The Quiet Devil

Terry D. Swain

TDS Publishers, Inc.
1945 Chestnut Log Drive, Suite 1
Lithia Springs, Ga 30122

Book Producer and text designer: TDS Publishers, Inc, Atlanta, GA
Proofreader: Katrina Thomas
Cover Designer: Daniel Harris, DanManz Design thedanmanz@gmail.com

ISBN: 9781099674020

DEDICATION

To anyone who is silently struggling with a secret vice or privately entangled in the grip of an isolated stronghold, and deeply desiring a way of escape to victory. This is book is dedicated to you.

CONTENTS

ACKNOWLEDGMENTS

I am eternally grateful to God for His love, wisdom and divine guidance. He has always been faithful and centered at the very core and essence of my life, orchestrating my steps with His sovereign hand. I'm deeply indebted to my family, my queen Natasha Swain, my daughter Halli and my son Jiar, for lending me to the world, to my life's purpose and to God's work. Without them, I would not be half of the man that I am today, nor would I have touched half of the lives that I've been blessed to encourage, equip and empower. This is the second book that I have written with the encouragement and support from so many people who believe in me and my calling to empower people to empower other people. Finally, a deep bow to all of those who have directly and indirectly supported, encouraged, challenged, and helped me to grow and become the vessel that I am. I am humbled to be a vessel, molded by God to pour into others what He, life and experience has poured into me.

PREFACE

"This is not your grandmother's devil."

Some people don't believe in devils, or the idea of devils, but I do.

I believe that devils exist and they are real.

However, I don't believe in the traditional, super-religious, horror movie idea of devils.

I don't believe that devils are ghostly and ghoulish figures that float around in the air scaring people. I choose to subscribe to a more comprehensible and spiritually-pragmatic approach to the concept of devils. I believe that they are spirits, invisible to the naked eye, whose purpose is not to scare people, but rather to deceive, distract, detour and even destroy people, if given the opportunity.

I have come to realize that one of the devil's greatest deceptions is convincing people they don't exist. In turn, this gives them the ability to go undetected as they move, inflicting devastation in a person's life.

When a person can't identify the work of the devil in their lives, it makes it that much more difficult to break free from wrongful behaviors, immoral habits and erroneous beliefs. While, on the other hand, there are those who do not want to accept responsibility for their wrong decisions or bad behaviors, and would rather blame it all on the devil. And that's a theological discourse that I have reserved for a later chapter, which is entitled "the devil made me do it".

This being the case, daily we encounter and battle devils, and more often than we even realize. Most people are unaware when a devil is even at work in their life, or in their mind to be more specific; and therein lays the problem. When a person doesn't believe in devils, or doesn't know how to identify a devil, they pass it off as something else other than what it really is. How many times have we passively dismissed seemingly small problems because we didn't think they had the potential to become something larger that demands our attention?

There is a verse in the Bible, **Song of Solomon 2:15**, which says *"it is the small foxes that spoil the vines."*

It is implying that those small and insignificant things, that we disregard and pass off as nothing, are the things that actually have the ability to cause the greatest harm and damage to us. It's not those big noticeable things that we can identify easily and quickly. But, it's those small, not easily detected, things that slowly and carefully eat away at our lives; without us ever realizing it, until the damage has been done and can't be reversed.

The saying goes, *"The chains of habit are usually to light to be felt, until they are too heavy to be broken"*. Most habits begin as an insignificant and harmless indulgence that grows into a heavy burden. No habit ever starts out as a burden. It takes time to grow and develop into the weighty proclivity. It starts off small, then gradually develops into a larger problem.

Take the large foxes for example. They don't destroy the vines or the vineyards. They only go after the visibly mature fruit, which hangs down on the vines. The larger foxes are also easier to spot. Because of their size, the vineyard keeper can detect them and run them away. The smaller foxes, on the other hand, are more difficult to spot. They attack the vine differently than the larger foxes. Since the small foxes can't reach the mature fruit, they nibble and eat away at the lower parts of the vines, which cuts off the flow of life and nutrients to the rest of the vines. This causes the fruits of the vine to tender quickly. Eventually, the ripened fruit falls to the ground where the smaller foxes can now eat them, destroying both fruit and vine. Not only do the small foxes destroy the fruit, they spoil the vine as well. Since, the vineyard keeper can't always detect the smaller foxes, they go undetected causing unseen and unfelt damage, which proves to be far greater and more destructive in the latter end.

In similar fashion, if you are not intentional about identifying and dealing with the seemingly small issues in your life, when you notice them, you are inevitably giving them permission to remain in your life. Inevitably, giving them permission to destroy your life as well.

Be aware that *the devil started out in the beginning as a snake in Genesis. But, in the end, he grew to become a dragon in Revelations.*

Adam and Eve were given the responsibility to guard, maintain and take care of the Garden of Eden, the same way we have been given the responsibility to guard our mind, heart and lives. They were not only responsible for keeping the garden pruned and healthy, they were also responsible for keeping out anything that would cause it damage or harm. It was their responsibility to keep it safe from harmful outside forces. But they allowed the snake, the devil, to remain in the garden. They did not believe the seemingly innocent snake had malicious intentions, or the ability to harm them. Since they did not deal with the snake in Genesis, it grew to become a more disastrous and destructive monster of a problem, later in Revelations. The problems we refuse to take care of and deal with don't just go away when we ignore them. They actually grow larger, stronger, and become more problematic.

It is dangerous to allow something to remain in your life, just because it seems small, harmless or insignificant; when it actually has malicious intentions and potentially disastrous consequences. Our disbelief and inability to identify demonic activity in our life leaves a blind spot for the devil to hide out and hang out in. And this is the one thing that separates the quiet devil from all other devils. It is what brands him the most destructive and dangerous devil of all. He is able to hide out in your life, when disregarded as a threat, or acknowledged as a problem that requires your immediate attention.

For this reason, he is labeled the quiet devil. He is very difficult to identify and very hard to recognize, until it is usually too late.

However, with God, it is never too late.

And that's why this book was written.

This book is not aimed at converting people from atheists and agnostics into believers. It is designed to help people define exactly what a devil is – and specifically the quiet devil. Exposing how and when he is at work in their life, and how to break free and remain free from the bondage of his grip. It forces us to look at and identify the unguarded and unprotected areas of our lives; those vulnerable areas that the quiet devil uses to gain access into our minds and into our belief systems.

This book is here to help break the grip of the mental stronghold that the quiet devil uses to put people in captivity and keep them in bondage to things like depression, sadness, anguish, guilt, suicide, and regret.

This book is here to empower and equip you with the information and the tools you need to stop the quiet devil from derailing your life and robbing it of the peace, joy, fulfillment and purpose that God has purposed you to have.

This book is written to expose and decode the lies and deception of how the quiet devil works and lurks, so you can avoid and escape his trappings, and keep your life on track.

Remember, this is not your grandmother's devil we are talking about. And we must deal with him in a real and relative way. We can't just pray him away. I believe in prayer, but not just prayer alone. We have a part to play in our prayers being answered. Prayer is just like faith, without works it is dead being alone. I believe in prayer and I also believe in action. They go together. We must get on our knees and pray, but we must get up on our feet and do the work. God has a part to play in our deliverance and we do also.

It is imperative that we uncover and unravel the nuances and strategies of the quiet devil - the devices that he uses to deceive and destroy. When we have this insight, we are better equipped to do our part in dethroning and rebuking him out of our lives.

This is a real devil, who is dangerous and crafty and waiting for the perfect opportunity to abolish your life, your family, your marriage, your children, your ministry, your business, your future, your finances, your health, your purpose and anything else he can get close enough to obliterate. *This is not your grandmother's devil!*

WHAT IS A QUIET DEVIL?

"The devil is not always roaring and vicious, often times he is polite and easy going."

So, what is a quiet devil? Is it a mute devil that can't speak? Is it a deaf devil that can't hear? Or, is it a shy devil that doesn't like attention?

Well, actually it is neither.

The quiet devil is a symbolic reference. A name that shouldn't be taken too literal. Quiet devil is simply a more colorful epithet that describes the true nature and character of this particular devil.

The term quiet relates more so to how it moves and operates, rather than how it expresses itself verbally. It is quiet in the nature of its soft and subtle tone.

It moves in silence and uses its subtlety as a disguise to deceive you into thinking that it is harmless and innocent. By definition, the quiet devil is

"An evil spirit, a mental disposition, which subtly and secretly forms a strong grip of bondage in a person's life, by hiding in the darkness of a lie that it has convinced a person to accept as truth."

The quiet devil is a very interesting devil and a very dangerous devil, which should be regarded as such. Unlike other devils, it is not obvious or apparent. Nooooo, it is not rambunctious or roaring. It is actually quite the opposite. It is polite and easy going. This is why I label it the "quiet" devil. It will not walk up to your front door, knock, and ask for permission to come in. It will not kick down the door and bombard its way in. No, that's not in its MO. The quiet devil is strategically silent, subtle and patient. It possesses the prowess of patience. It is never hasty or in a rush. It is actually reserved and introverted. It hides out for extensive lengths of time, constructing its stronghold, waiting for the most inopportune time to reveal its true intentions. And that my friend is his strong suit, having the ability to sneak in quietly and undetected, set up its stronghold and wreak havoc in your life before you ever recognize its presence.

In the same way the mass shooters go undetected until the ticking time bomb explodes; so does the quiet devil. Whenever a reporter interviews the family members and peers of a mass shooter, the story is always the same. They were quiet, polite, reserved, anti-social and easy-going. They were never loud, popular, outgoing or socially confident.

The quiet devil fits the same profile of a mass-murderer, and his intentions are the same as well. He goes undetected and under the radar the entire time, until the sudden outburst of uncontrolled fury is unleashed. No one ever recognizes the quiet easy-going guy as mass-murderer, until it is too late. It's only after the damage has been done that his profile is compiled and recognized.

It is in fact the quiet devil who is behind the deceptive ideology of a mass-murder. The quiet devil was able to quietly creep into the dark recesses of the mass-murderers mind and convince him to accept a lie as truth. The lie is usually a justification and rationalization for killing his innocent and defenseless victims. Convincing them to believe that the people they murder deserve to die, when that is indeed a lie straight from the pits of hell. But somewhere the quiet devil gained access into the attackers minds. Usually, it is through racist or nationalist groups and internet sites that promote their same twisted ideology, claiming that the people they are killing are to blame for some loss or deprivation they are experiencing. All the while, the gunmen are camouflaged under the guise of a quiet, polite well-mannered demeanor. Out of sight and out of mind. Off the radar.

It is in that quietness, in that seclusion of privacy, that the person finally emerges out of the darkness into the light and shoots innocent school children, randomly fire into a crowd of unsuspecting people at a concert, or shoots up a church sanctuary during a Bible study. Unsuspected and undetected. *The devil is not always roaring and vicious, often times he is polite and easy going.*

TERRY D. SWAIN

THE SQUATTER

"God knocks on the front door, but the devil sneaks in through the back door."

The quiet devil doesn't show up in your life blatant and obvious. Neither does it show up ranting and raving. That's not its style. It prefers to subtly sneak into the dark secluded recesses of your mind, and plant the evil and wicked seeds of deception and lies. It gains access to your life secretly, builds trust, and then sits comfortably out of the way. It patiently waits, allowing the roots of its lies to sink slowly and deeply into place without notice.

This can only happen when we neglect to safeguard those vulnerable and unstable areas of our lives. We all have those unoccupied territories and neglected spaces within us that have not been filled, nor labeled as either good or bad, right or wrong. They are the unattended and unsettled areas in our belief systems, which we call convictions. Usually, they are those grey areas that we are still on the fence about.

Like the married guy who thinks there is nothing wrong with a little harmless flirting on the job, until he flirts too much with the wrong woman and finds himself in a full blown affair. By the time he realizes that he has gone too far, it is often too late and he is in over his head. When he decides to end the affair, he can't... Why? Because his lover threatens to expose him. His lust has blinded him from seeing the truth. He bought and believed the lie that he could trust her, and left himself vulnerable, giving her the tools to destroy him. She now has the receipts and the ammunition to use against him... the infamous penis pics, the sexually explicit text messages,

FaceTime screen shots, secret recordings, and much more.

Now, he is under the grip of her extortion and coercion, which could have been prevented, had he set the necessary boundaries of his conviction in place in the beginning. He now detests and despises what he once desired. He now hates and abhors what he once hungered for. And now, the stronghold is set in place, and he is now trapped inside of the lie.

This type of outcome is not only relegated to a cheating spouse, but anyone can be susceptible to the devil's deceptive lure. And the common factor in the equation is having loose and unsettled convictions. You can't be neutral and take a firm stand against temptation, lustful tendencies and immoral desires. It's impossible. You have to have a firm stance.

Until you set sure conclusions on your convictions, and categorize them as either good or bad, you leave open a space and opportunity for the devil to sneak into your life. Unfortunately, the devil is not a gentleman like God who comes in to our situations by invitation. God doesn't come into our lives unannounced, nor does He sneak in through a back door. He politely knocks.

Revelations 3:20 says, *"Behold, I stand at the door, and knock: if any man hears My voice, and opens the door, I will come in to him, and will sup with him, and he with Me."*

God knocks on the door to our heart. He knocks on the door to our lives, and then He waits for us to open the door to invite Him in. He doesn't just barge in.

The devil, on the other hand, is an intruder. He will either force his way in, or more subtly, like the quiet devil, find a way to sneak in to our lives, gaining access by secrecy or trickery.

One of the sure indicators that something or someone is not good for you is the way it enters your life. If something or someone has to access your life through secrecy and privacy, then chances are it is not of God. The only reason someone would want to access your life through a private entrance is because they have something to hide. It's the same reason someone would enter your home through the back door, when the front door works perfectly fine. They don't want to be seen or noticed. They do not want their true intentions and motives to be revealed. A burglar prefers the back door, because he has dangerous and clandestine intentions that he wants to conceal.

Private communications and secret conversations are often the back doors by which many dangerous things and people gain access into our lives. They are the same back doors that we willingly and carelessly open for the quiet devil to enter into, when we have the wrong set of beliefs or unsettled convictions.

If we don't close those back doors, then the deceptive voices that enter can influence us to bend to the wrong side of our convictions.

In the same way that many Christians, recklessly believe church teachings, without knowing why they believe them. Their child like faith and immaturity will accept and believe ideologies based on incorrect or incomplete interpretations from preachers and ill-informed pastors.

This type of thinking doesn't leave a person with much of a foundation to stand on. Neither does it leave them with any real defense against the quiet devil. This blind kind of faith has contributed greatly to the destruction of many people of faith.

Once confronted with situations that contradict what they have blindly believed, they are unable to stand strong and defend their faith. So the brittle foundation of their convictions gives way under the weight of temptations, which leaves an open back door for the quiet devil to creep in through.

Any space left unoccupied or ignored is available for residence. When a person is indecisive and reluctant to make determinations on unsettled issues, it leaves the unclaimed space up for grabs.

The quiet devil's strategy is much like the law of squatting, which says if you own a home, but don't live in it, someone else can sneak into the property and live there unaware.

Squatting is when someone deliberately enters the property of another and lives there, or intends to claim residence, without the owner's permission.

For many inattentive and unsuspecting people, that's exactly what's happening in their lives right now. They are allowing the quiet devil access to inhabit areas of their life, without permission. This is why the Word of God instructs us to watch as well as pray. It is not enough to just pray. We must be intentionally attentive, watching what goes on in front of our eyes, what passes between our ears, what passes through our mind, and what enters into our spirit.

Like the squatter, the quiet devil is kicked back with his feet up, lounging in that unattended space, scheming and plotting to gain possession and set up a stronghold in that area of your life.

A squatter has legal allowance to use the property of another in the absence of an attempt by the owner to force eviction. But how can the owner force an eviction, when the owner is not aware that someone is residing there. And, that is the problem that the quiet devil creates, by secretly and subtly gaining access to space in your mind that you haven't given him permission to, nor God for that matter. How can a person rebuke or remove something from their lives, when they don't know it is there?

Squatters are often able to claim rights over the spaces they squat in by virtue of occupation, rather than ownership. This means a devil has a right to occupy the space in your mind even though you own it. They don't own the space, but they occupy it, since you are not using it. Squatting is similar to (*and potentially a necessary condition of*) adverse possession, where a possessor of real property without title may eventually gain legal title to the real property.

The devil, like the squatter, can attempt to gain legal right to the unoccupied space when he has lived in that space over an extended period of time.

When we place a conviction, based on the truth of God's Word, on those neutral issues in our lives, it is in essence a legal title of ownership to those spaces. We give God the title, or entitlement, to reside in those areas whenever we base and settle our convictions on the principles from the Word of God. Once we give the ownership over to the right convictions, the Holy Spirit can now occupy it and it is no longer vacant or susceptible to squatting devils.

Like the squatter, once a quiet devil has secretly squatted in our mind for a certain period of time, he works undetected constructing and setting up the space to accommodate his purpose. That purpose is to build a stronghold.

Strongholds are not set up overnight. It takes time to set them up. No one becomes an addict overnight. No one gets entangled in an adulterous affair overnight. No one falls into a state of depression overnight. No one becomes a pedophile overnight. No one becomes a criminal overnight. It takes time to construct these things, and this is why the devil takes his time; making sure that he lays the foundation of his entrenchment strong and deep.

For this reason specifically, the enemy has to be "quiet" and has to go undetected when operating in your life. If he is not quiet, you will be able to identify him and disarm him before the addiction, affair, depression, etc. has a chance to set in. This approach makes it difficult for a person to break free from certain behaviors, addictions and tendencies.

A squatter or quiet devil is considered a trespasser that has no rights, if detected in the early stages. This is why it is extremely important to identify and deal with him as soon as possible. It's only when the property is abandoned, and someone has "squatted" on it for a statutory period, usually a number of years, can the squatter gain control of the premises.

Once you realize there is a problem, it must be addressed immediately. According to squatter laws, if the rightful owner effectively removes the squatter's access, even temporarily during the statutory period, the squatter loses the benefit of that possession. If a squatter, i.e. *a quiet devil*, has claimed rights over an unsettled conviction in your mind and set up residence, i.e. *a stronghold*, then it is your responsibility to remove him.

It is very difficult to get untangled from the quiet devils grip, once he has setup residence for a prolonged period of time. However, there is hope. Freedom and deliverance can be found through Gods Word and applying these practical truths that I will be sharing with you.

You can be free and delivered; both of which I am going to show you how to obtain, throughout the course of this book. I will show how to be free - completely free, and how to maintain that freedom by locking the door on the devil, so you never get entangled again. *God knocks on the front door, but the devil sneaks in through the back door.*

THE SNAKE IN THE WATER PUDDLE

"The devil rests comfortably in the problems we refuse to fix".

It was a gorgeous summer day. The window blinds were pulled open in every room, and beaming rays of sun were shining into the house. I opened the front door, stepped out on to the porch, and was overwhelmed with the crisp morning air and the brightness of the morning sun. I'd just mowed the lawn the evening before, and the smell of fresh cut grass was still resting lightly in the air. It seemed like the perfect summer morning. Then suddenly, out of the corner of my eye, I saw something moving in the grass along the edge of the yard. I must have startled it when I opened the door. I rushed to the edge of the porch to get a closer look. I couldn't see anything, but I heard something moving on the ground. It scrambled away into the woods ruffling leaves as it moved.

I immediately thought to myself, 'that had to be a snake'. I'd never seen a snake that close to the house before, and it concerned me. I wondered, where did it come from? Is it poisonous? Are there more snakes, and what do I need to do to prevent it from coming back? I couldn't shake the thought of a snake being that close to my house; to my family.

I began to think of possible reasons why it would be in that particular area of the grass, and the only reasonable explanation I could come up with was a puddle of water that was located only a few feet away from the area it fled from. The snake was probably resting in the puddle of water, cooling off. But, when it heard me walking on the porch, it hurried away into the woods. The puddle had been there for a while. It was an accumulation of water created from a leaking pipe that I had neglected to fix.

The leak was coming from a pipe fitting on the base of the outdoor water faucet, and it was leaking underground. On several occasions, I had attempted to dig it up and repair it, but my efforts were always superficial. I wasn't really a handyman. I just did the bare minimum to repair it, and it always came undone again. But now, I realized that if the puddle was the reason for the snake's visitation, I had to fix it properly, and fix it soon.

For the rest of the day, whenever I went in or out of the house, I was thinking about that damned snake. I would look out into that direction of the yard and check to see if the snake had returned. I went to bed thinking about it, dreamt about it, and even woke up the next morning with it still fresh on my mind. The next morning, I got out of bed, walked to the front door and quietly and gently opened the door. If the snake was there, I didn't want to startle it like I'd done the day before. I peeked my head out slowly, and just as I had suspected, there it was again, coiled up and resting; sunbathing in the puddle of water. It was just chilling there, comfortably, like it was at home.

I stepped out on to the porch and stomped my feet loudly to scare it away. It fled just as it did the day before, into the woods across the leaves. It was now clearer than ever, the problem had to be fixed, immediately! So I grabbed a shovel and a pick, and dug up the ground around the area of the pipe where the leak was. I took pictures of the fittings and the pipes that needed to be replaced and I left for the hardware store. The owner of the store helped me to find everything I needed to repair the waterline, and he also gave me some helpful tips. I worked tirelessly until I fixed the leak completely. After I fixed the leak, the water puddle eventually receded and the snake never returned.

Like the snake in the water puddle, whenever we have leaks in our life, they create a space for the enemy, *the quiet devil,* to rest in. A leak can be a child rebelling against parental authority, a teenager drifting into peer pressure, a health symptom that you keep ignoring, or even the mismanagement of funds. Leaks are what I consider unresolved issues, undealt with sins, or areas of weakness in our lives that we do nothing about. They are the issues that we allow to go unattended and unaddressed without taking a proactive approach to regulate them, but rather a reactive approach. We have a tendency to ignore problems, until they get to a point where they demand our attention. I made the same mistake with how I mishandled the issue with the water leak. I ignored it, until it attracted a snake. Only after I was faced with the threat of danger did I move to action. This simple truth echoes in the lives of so many people. It isn't until the problem threatens our lives, or grows out of control that we give it the attention it needs. We must begin to take a proactive stance to address the leaks in our lives, instead of waiting until they require our attention.

If you are passive and uninformed on how to deal with devils, destructive habits and evil proclivities, you will do the same thing I did with the leaky faucet. You will not fix the root of the problem, you will just do the bare minimum to repair it or just cover it temporarily. If you do not fix it properly, it is just put off to be dealt with another day. It's like putting a bandage on a cut that needs medical attention. The bandage doesn't solve the problem. It just hides the problem.

When issues are not attended to immediately, correctly and completely, you leave an opportunity and a place for the quiet devil to return. As long as I continued to provide short-term solutions to the leaky pipe, it continued to come undone, creating the same problem over and over again. Once I took the proper actions to resolve the problem, the puddle receded and the snake had nothing to return to. The sooner we correct problems, the better. Since I was able to detect the snake early on, I was able to address the problem and fix it once and for all. After I removed the leak that was creating the puddle, the snake had nothing to return to.

After the snake and the water leak ordeal, I realized that there was a lesson to be learned. A lesson that I could use to help others avoid and escape the same dangers I'd faced and overcame. The snake and the quiet devil are both seeking to inhabit and occupy space that doesn't belong to them. As I battled with the snake to reclaim control over the ground, the space that it was trying to occupy, I realized that the quiet devil does the same thing. Except, he wants the space in our minds. We must fight for the space that he wants to inhabit. We have to be courageous, confrontational and vigilant. We can't be afraid, passive or dismissive. The same way that I approached and resolved the situation with the snake, is the same way you must also address the issues in your life. *The devil rests comfortably in the problems we refuse to fix.* Fix the problem!

SILENT BUT DEADLY

"The quiet conscience is an invention of the devil."

We often associate quietness with innocence, when in most cases it is quite the contrary. Just because a person is quiet that doesn't mean they are innocent, and just because something is silent that doesn't mean it is harmless. When in reality, those who are the quietest can be, and are often the most dangerous.

Growing up as a teenager in my hometown, Alpine Alabama, my brother was one of the most feared, respected and notorious gangsters in our neighborhood. He was a mysterious gangster figure, and an almost living legend in the eyes of those who lived outside of our town. This was before the age of online technology and social media. People didn't know who he was, they just heard stories about him. He rarely left out of the radius of the neighborhood, but whenever he did leave, there was always another story that followed him back. He was a quiet gangster who moved in silence, and people feared and respected his quietness and silence. Most people were braggadocios and loud, but not my brother. When he made up in his mind to retaliate on rival gangs or commit any acts of crime, he wouldn't advertise it or send messages about what he was going to do. He wouldn't say a word but he would act suddenly with surprise. No words to warn or caution his enemies. Much like the quiet devil, he moves in silence, and catches his subjects off guard and unexpected. It was the subtlety of the snake that allowed it to get close enough to Eve and engage in intimate conversation. It was the subtlety of the snake that allowed it to get close to my home and take up residence in the water puddle.

Those who are quiet can use the guise of quietness to hide their evil motives and intentions to get close to people. It is quietness that gives evil the ability to build trust with its victims, then hide and go undetected, until it is close enough to strike a fatal blow.

The camouflage of silence can cover evil in plain sight.

Take the viper for instance. It can hide its venomous subtlety, allowing it to get close enough to its prey to strike without warning or notice. It is stealthy and calculating. It is able to slide up to its prey silently without notice, going undetected and unnoticed until positioned perfectly and close enough to strike.

How often do molesters go unnoticed in households that seem to be healthy and nurturing? How often do racists hide under the cloak of a reserved and honest persona? How often does a serial killer blend in to a community as a quiet neighbor who doesn't bother anyone? How often does a thief turn out to be a polite and seemingly nice young man who you'd never suspect? Or, how often do bad girls masquerade as daddy's little princesses, when in fact they are very promiscuous and sexually active.

Like the viper, evil can take on many shapes and appearances, hiding out in plain sight, undetected.

Such is the case of the quiet devil.

He could be secretly forming a dangerous plan in the mind of someone close to you, while you have no idea of the terrible and evil plans that are being formulated.

As a reminder, our working definition for the quiet devil is:

"An evil spirit, a mental disposition, which subtly and secretly forms a strong grip of bondage in a person's life, by hiding in the darkness of a lie that it has convinced a person to accept as truth."

It is able to subtly and secretly sneak in and build a strong grip in a person's life, without notice because of our inability to see the quiet thoughts in a person's mind. Quiet thoughts are the unnoticeable brainwork and unrecognizable reasoning that isn't revealed by expression.

There are instances when we are able to tell what a person is thinking by their facial expression or body language. But quiet thoughts have no discernable expressions. They can't be detected.

Quietness and patience are the two greatest attributes that the quiet devil possesses. They give him the ability to conceal his true nature and intentions, for extended periods of time.

Albert Einstein said that *the quiet conscience is an invention of the devil.* Truer words have rarely ever been spoken. It is that idle quietness of the mind that gives way to the devil. Those who give their mind idly to quietness are targets for the devil's work. An idle mind is indeed the devil's workshop.

Silence can be deadly, when we choose not to speak what we truly feel. In fact, quiet people usually have the most to say but they conceal it and never open up to anyone. The silence eventually turns into inner turmoil, which leads to irrational thinking and behavior because it was never God's intent for us to conceal our thoughts. He knows that concealed thoughts can be poisonous to the soul. They fester and breed anger, hate, resentment, grudges, stress, anxiety, depression, regret, anguish and much more. Without an outlet, the quiet devil is able to create a monster inside of us. A monster that desensitizes a person to reasoning and makes it difficult to look themselves in the eyes without seeing shame and disgrace.

The deadly silence of an evil scheming conscious is dangerous. A frightful place, where something horrific could be brewing, undetected and unattended. Until it finally spills over. *The quiet conscious is an invention of the devil.*

THE CORNER OF THE ROOFTOP

"Quiet thoughts are the hardest thoughts to control."

The first chapter of The Gospel of Matthew tells the story of Jesus' birth. It also gives some insight on how the quiet devil can gain access into a person's thoughts. In this case, how he gained access into the life of Jesus' step-father, Joseph.

Jesus' mother, Mary, was pledged to be married to Joseph. But before they came together in marriage, she was found to be pregnant through the Holy Spirit. The baby Jesus was not Joseph's biological son, and this was the vulnerable point of entry for the quiet devil. Since, Joseph wasn't Jesus' biological father, the devil went to work on Joseph's emotions, fears and pride, by whispering thoughts of both suspicion and shame. I imagine that Joseph thought about what his family and friends were thinking. He wondered what people were saying behind his back.

Since Joseph was faithful to the law, he wanted to do the honorable and noble thing and stay with Mary. He really did not want to expose Mary to public disgrace and humiliation. But, now the quiet devil has planted seeds in his mind and he is quietly and privately contemplating leaving Mary. Knowing he was not Jesus' biological father bothered him internally. Joseph never said a word to anyone else. He just simply wrestled with his concealed thoughts within himself. He did not talk to anyone about the dark thoughts he was having. He did not seek counseling or advice from anyone about what he should do. He carried the weight of his emotions and inner turmoil alone.

And like Joseph, there are countless men and women, right now, who are physically present in their home with their wife and children, living what seems to be a normal life, while silently contemplating divorce. They are not just contemplating divorce, they are also quietly and privately planning how they are going to carry it out. They are strategizing a path of escape. And while there are countless spouses who are on the edge of giving up and walking away from their marriage and family, there are just as many who have already walked away. Men and women who have suddenly, without notice, abandoned their spouses unexpectedly and unsuspectedly.

Recall, Joseph *had in mind* to divorce Mary privately. He did not tell Mary or anyone else that he was thinking about leaving. He just kept them in his mind. Closed off from the rest of the world, he was living his life as he normally would - going about his daily routines while everyone else was unaware of what was really going on inside of his head. And that is the mental space that the quiet devil uses to hide out in.

It is in that secluded mental space where he convinces a husband to believe that his identity is no longer valued or honored in a relationship. And the quiet devil now has him right where he wants him.

I like to call that secluded mental space *"the corner of the rooftop"*. The corner of the rooftop is a quiet, secluded place, away from everyone else. It is a place of escape from everyone and everything. In ancient Israel, the architectural style of homes had flat rooftops. The rooftop was the highest point of the house, elevated above the noise and activity that goes on under the roof. The husband could retreat to the rooftop to get away from whatever was going on inside of the house.

The corner of the house top represents his place of withdrawal and disengagement. A place of quietness and peace.

One of the wise sayings of King Solomon, **Proverbs 21:9** says *"It is better to dwell in the corner of the rooftop, than to dwell in an open* *house with a nagging or brawling woman"*. This implies that a husband would rather be in the quiet small space, alone, rather than remain in a wide open space with a loud nagging wife.

Men are creatures of habit, habitat and habitation. A man needs his natural space and domain. A space that he occupies as his own. He needs his own personal space that belongs to him, and him alone. A place and space that he can withdraw to, in seclusion, just be alone to process his thoughts and zone out. A getaway. A place of retreat.

It can be a man cave, a garage, a shop, a home office, a studio, or a garden. It can even be activities like hunting, sports or video games. It can be whatever and wherever he chooses. But he needs some activity or some place that belongs to him exclusively.

The corner of the rooftop can be a physical place or any of many extracurricular activities. Anything that keeps him away from the nagging woman. Anything that temporarily takes his mind off of the current stress and strain of his relationship.

His home is where he retreats from the world, but where does he retreat to when he needs some time away from home. The home is not his space alone, because he occupies it with his wife or significant other and/or his children. It doesn't belong to just him. So when the woman begins to nag, relationship pressure begins to build, and he feels as if he can't think, breathe, or hear his own thoughts. He needs his space away from home, or a space at home that's away from everything and everyone else. A space that belongs exclusively to him.

In biblical days, a man's place of retreat was the rooftop. His own small personal piece of peace. If a man doesn't have that personal space to retreat to, and if he does not choose carefully his place of solace and solitude, he can find it in the wrong place or the wrong person.

For many of the men who do not have that place of retreat at home, they often retreat to spending extra hours at their job, hanging out at the local bar, hanging out with the guys or even at worse, they find it in the company of another woman.

The corner of the rooftop can also be a mental or emotional place that a man resorts to in his mind. This happens when he shuts down and refuses to communicate or express himself verbally. When a woman begins to nag, her man may not say anything verbally, but he's telling her off in his head. He may not be saying anything with his mouth, but he is cussing her out in his mind. This is when he has retreated to the corner of the rooftop. When he shuts down and becomes quiet and distant. It's a dangerous space to be in when a person holds in negative feelings and thoughts. If you don't express how you feel, be it good or bad, that's pressure building up, which makes you susceptible to the quiet devil.

The corner of the rooftop is beneficial when it is used for its rightful purpose. But it can be very harmful, destructive and damaging when used or abused for evil purposes.

Like King David, in the story of **2 Samuel 11**. He was on the rooftop of his home and saw another man's wife bathing. He thought she was very beautiful and he sent for her to be brought unto him. He committed adultery with the woman and conspired to have her husband killed. All of this as a result of him being alone on his rooftop.

Even though the rooftop is an escape from chaos and conflict, if a man is in a vulnerable and unstable state of mind, it can easily and quickly turn into a place of cheating, lies and deception. The place where you retreat to for peace, could potentially create greater turmoil. See, it is also in the corner of the rooftop of a man's mind where he starts quietly building irrational plans to escape from his current circumstances. This was the same thing that Joseph was doing when he was secretly planning to divorce Mary. When a man suddenly ups and leaves his wife and family, when a Pastor suddenly ups and leaves his church, or any other responsibilities and commitments that he has obligated himself to; it leaves people shocked and thinking *"where did that come from, I had no idea"*.

Though it seemed spontaneous, it didn't come suddenly. It was something that had been brewing all along, but it was just concealed.

A man needs a peaceful space to retreat to. A space where he can express himself without consequence. That space is usually alone with his own thoughts, or around other men who can mutually relate with his issues. *A woman should be a man's quiet place.* She should calm the raging storm inside of him, not stir it up. When a man's expressions are counteracted repeatedly with emotional confrontation from his woman, eventually he shuts down and retreats to his mental man cave – the rooftop of his mind.

Then, the quiet devil takes advantage of that opportunity and joins him there on the rooftop - when he is most vulnerable - in solitude and silence. It is in that solitude and silence where he builds bombs, ticking time bombs, just waiting to detonate. Eventually, exploding and killing and injuring the lives of all who are in its path of destruction. *Quiet thoughts are the hardest thoughts to control.*

TERRY D. SWAIN

THE UNDER CURRENT

"Beware of friendly exteriors that hide evil intentions".

When I was about fourteen years old, I was playing with my brothers and a few of our cousins at the bank of a lake near our home. We were standing ankle deep in the edge of the water with our pants legs rolled up to our knees, laughing and playing. For some reason I decided to be a daredevil and walk out further into the water. I felt the bank declining the further I walked out, until the water was almost up to my waist. I took another step and suddenly my foot slipped and a quick and powerful force almost snatched me beneath the water. There was a powerful and cold undercurrent flowing just below the calm surface of the water. My life briefly flashed before my eyes. I saw myself being submerged under water and being swept away down the lake. I saw myself struggling underwater holding my breath and swinging my arms wildly to break free from the grip of the under current. I imagined myself miraculously popping up out of the water, catching a hold of a tree branch that was leaning over into the water as I used it to pull myself to safety.

Breathing heavy and totally exasperated from the thought of what could have happened, I hurried out of the water and collapsed on the ground. Lying on my back looking up at the sky, I just laid there thanking God. I looked over at everyone else and they were still playing and laughing, and no one had even noticed what just happened to me.

I was experiencing one of the most frightening experiences of my life, and no one was even aware that I was going through it. This is often the case with people who are struggling with a stronghold, a crisis, an addiction, or any sin or situation that has them entangled. People rarely are aware when other people are silently struggling with something.

Every day, there are people who are struggling with things that have pulled them under and overwhelmed their lives while no one else is even aware. People too often go through silent and secluded struggles alone, simply because people are either not aware of other people's silent battles or don't recognize what others are going through. They either don't care what others are going through or they are just too busy dealing with their own lives to get involved with what others are going through.

The undercurrent is like the ulterior motives of people, which hide underneath a pleasant face. It doesn't jump out at you and grab you. No, it lures you in and then sucks you under. It goes undetected and waits until you step into it. Some people are good at hiding their true motives and intentions until they get what they really want.

How often are thirsty men seduced and lead blindly astray by the facade of a woman's superficial exterior? Only to find themselves entangled in the undercurrent of poor judgment and regret.

How often are vulnerable women deceived by the smooth talking game of a man, who only wants sex, and nothing else to do with them? Only to find themselves drowning in the misery of heartache and disappointment.

How many times have young boys been seduced by the shallow allure of crime and drugs? Only to have the undercurrent of fast living and fast money snatch them away from their family; sucking them into a lonely and remorseful life of incarceration.

All a result of the consequences of flirting too close or too much with danger.

Unaware of the raging undercurrent beneath the surface, the danger goes unnoticed, until you step too far over into it. Then, before you know it, you're in over your head, struggling to break free from a gripping addiction, an unhealthy relationship, a terrible habit, a criminal lifestyle, or an adulterous affair. You find yourself fighting like hell to resurface from the mess you've gotten yourself into. But, with every stroke you take to fight your way back to the surface, it seems like you can't break free. You begin to think,

"What have I gotten myself into?"
"How did I let things go this far?"
"I knew better."
"I should have stopped while I had the chance."

Like my fourteen year old self, we often play to close to danger without realizing it. We test the limits of our safety, taking risks with temptations, trying to see how far we can go without getting caught up.

Temptation is deceptively sneaky. It begins subtly. Like the cashier worker taking a few dollars here and there out of the register. Incrementally, taking more money, more frequently. Eventually, the cashier becomes reckless and careless, going for the big take. Only to find herself in too far and too deep to turn around. Eventually, the manager notices the money missing on the financial reports and tracks it back to the dishonest cashier who is eventually fired, prosecuted and sued. Temptation begins as an adolescent casually experimenting with gateway drugs like marijuana. In the beginning, it is a social pass time with friends. Then, it gradually evolves into harder drugs like molly, cocaine and heroin. Before the user is even aware of its grip, they are sucked under into the undercurrent of a consuming addiction.

An undercurrent is a subsurface current of water that flows beneath the surface undetected, much like the hidden opinions, feelings, or tendencies that people hide beneath the surface. *Still waters run deep.* On the surface appearing peaceful and harmless, while something more dangerous and sinister is flowing just shortly beneath the exterior. For this reason, we should not take things at face value. You can't always trust things that are obvious. When something doesn't feel right, chances are it may not be right. You have to trust your gut feeling.

The primary deception of the quiet devil is to take your focus away from the underlying danger while keeping your attention and focus on what's obvious on the surface. In the story that I shared about the snake and the water puddle, the puddle was created by a leak that was underground. The problem was not the obvious puddle that formed on top of the ground. The puddle on the surface was a secondary consequence. The real problem was the leak that slowly dripped beneath the ground, which was the root cause. The puddle wasn't the real problem. The real problem was the leak that formed the puddle. When people are displaying obvious signs of turmoil on the surface, it's because there is something broken inside of them, beneath the surface. *The external symptom is just an indicator of an internal problem.*

I could have drained the puddle every day but it would have continued to return. We fail to face and fix issues in our lives when we attempt to address the visible results and not the unseen factors that are causing the issues. To fix the reoccurring problems in our lives, we do not address what's manifesting on the surface. We have to address the root of the problem, the deeper issue that's going on beneath the surface. We have to fix the leaks.

The real issue is not the defiant child that's acting out. It is the reason *why* the child is acting out. What is causing the child to act out?

The real issue isn't the young girl's promiscuity. It is the reason *why* she is being promiscuous. What is causing her to be promiscuous?

The real issue isn't the hoarders clutter. It is the reason *why* they created the clutter. What is causing them to hoard?

The real problem is not "what" a person is doing, it is "why" the person is doing it. What is the root cause? If we deal with the why, then we will inevitably be able to control the what.

It's the same with curing a health issue. To cure the problem, you do not treat the symptoms, you treat what's causing the symptoms. To lower your cholesterol you have to stop eating foods that increase your cholesterol. To prevent diabetic symptoms you have to stop eating foods with high levels of sugar. It's inexpensive and easier to purchase and eat the bad foods that cause disease and health issues than it is to purchase and take the medicine that helps control the sickness. Simply put, you have to stop stepping into the undercurrent. Our food is our medicine. The answer to the underlying problem is found in eating the right foods.

It's like the grave reality of my mother's simple but profound wisdom that my mother often told me and my brothers. She would say, *"Trouble is easy to get into but it is hard to get out of"*. Whenever we disregarded her words of wisdom, like a self-fulfilling prophecy, we would always find ourselves trapped in the consequences of our bad decisions – the under current. And this is the reality of most people who allow themselves to be deceived by the silent but deadly deception of the quiet devil.

Allowing sinful behavior to continue, can, and inevitably will, remove you totally from the will of God, your purpose and your destiny. It will cause your life to succumb to the devastation and destruction of the under current, which is the quiet devil's stronghold. Don't be fooled! Just because something or someone appears peaceful and good on the surface, that doesn't mean that their intentions are good. The calm and pleasant exterior is often a mask to hide what's really inside. *Beware of friendly exteriors that hide evil intentions.*

TERRY D. SWAIN

THE LOUD SILENCE

"The quietest people have the loudest minds."

The Loud Silence is anything that can be sensed or detected by visual observation, but goes unacknowledged. It is usually those inklings we feel, but typically ignore or disregard. They are the vibes ore energy we pick up on, but can't quite put our finger on what it is. Most people acknowledge it after the fact by saying things like, *"something told me"*, *"I had a feeling"*, or *"I knew something was wrong"*.

The loud silence is the unexpressed emotions and unspoken thoughts that people hold and conceal inside of their minds, which tend to go ignored until it finally reaches a tipping point and explodes. Like the killer who shot up the Tree of Life Synagogue in Pittsburgh. Like the gunman who shot up the Marjory Stoneman Douglas High School in Parkland, Florida, or Dylan Roof the shooter in the Charleston Church Massacre.

After each of these senseless executions, the attackers were all profiled as quiet and reserved people who went under the radar. Yet, when family, friends and neighbors of the shooters were interviewed, the running theme was the same. Everyone admitted that they knew something wasn't right, or they saw traits that hinted at the fact that these were troubled individuals. But no one ever said anything. There was something loud and troubling going on inside of the minds of these shooters but since they kept it concealed, others who observed or interacted with them were unable to identify exactly what it was. They knew something was off but couldn't quite put their fingers on it, until it was too late. Bear in mind, *the devil is not always roaring and vicious, often times he is polite and easy going.* They had loud voices and loud thoughts blasting in their mind, even though they never expressed them outwardly. *Evil is not always obvious*; often it is hiding and unrecognizable. Quiet even.

I've come to learn from the mass shooting profiles that *the quietest people have the loudest minds.* Those who don't say a lot are the ones who think a lot. Those who are the quietest on the outside are the ones who have the most going on in the inside. And when those loud thoughts have been trapped inside for extended periods of time without an outlet, they spill over and are expressed through violent out lashes. *The thoughts that are never spoken out of the mouth are usually screamed in the mind.* Those who are not brave enough to say what they feel with their mouth, usually express it with their actions.

Mark 1:21-27 tells the story of a quiet reserved man who was possessed with a devil. The man attended weekly services in a particular synagogue, where Jesus had come to teach. The man who was possessed with the devil had sat quietly in the synagogue for many years going unnoticed and undetected by the leaders and the regular attendees. Until the day that Jesus visited as a guest preacher. As Jesus was teaching the light and truth of His Words exposed the devil. The devil began to violently cry out of the quiet man. He was begging Jesus to leave him alone. After Jesus exposed the devil, He went on to cast him out of the man. All of the people were astonished and amazed when they saw Jesus cast the devil out of the man.

It is interesting to note that the people were amazed at Jesus casting out the devil, but were not amazed at the fact that the devil was hiding and residing quietly, undetected and comfortable, in the Temple for so long. This speaks to a lack of discernment within the church and the lives of people who we interact with on a regular basis. They saw this man every week in the Temple gatherings. Someone should have noticed a devil in the house of God. This tells me that the devil had sat there throughout the years, unaffected by their many sermons, prayers and singing that took place weekly in the building.

I wonder how many people are currently going through the motions of Churchanity, life, work or family, while quietly struggling with a devil.

How many people are so deeply entangled within the struggle of a vice or addiction but too afraid to cry out for help?

How many people are silently trapped in a fortified situation, alone, while others aren't even aware of what they are going through?

There was obviously no power in the redundant, routine, religious rituals of their synagogue because something should have agitated or convicted the devil. However, it wasn't until Jesus showed up with the true power that the devil was immediately cast out.

Not only is the building, where we worship God considered the Temple but our individual bodies are considered to be God's Temples as well. We must be careful of what we allow into our bodies. The quiet devil not only sits unbothered in the four-walled temples of the Church, but he will also sit unbothered in our bodily temples if we let him. Whenever you participate in sinful practices or evil tendencies and never feel convicted, guess who is sitting silently inside the temple of your mind?

You guessed it. The quiet devil.

If you are not using your spiritual discernment, you will not even notice him. The same way that the people in the synagogue didn't notice him. The same way that the people in Emmanuel A.M.E. Church of Charleston, SC didn't notice him. The same way the people in the Tree of Life Synagogue in Pittsburgh did not notice him, until it was too late. They disregarded him as a threat to their safety because he appeared quiet and harmless.

Just because something is quiet or polite that doesn't mean that it is harmless. When a person is quiet, that's when you should be most concerned. Those who are the quietest are actually the most dangerous. These were all quiet, reserved but troubled men who carried out these mass shootings. Columbine High School, Virginia College and the Aurora Movie Theatre were all shot up by men who gave in to the loud silence in their heads.

It's not the loud dog with the big bark that you have to worry about, it's the quiet dog that doesn't bark and attacks without warning. It's often those little quiet things in our lives that cause the most damage.

It is *the small foxes spoil the vine*, not the large foxes. *The large foxes go straight for the fruit, while the little foxes go for the root.* The vine inevitably withers and dies, no longer able to produce fruit again. The small foxes are able to do more damage because they go undetected, unnoticed and under the radar due to their small stature.

When a dog is barking you know where it is, how far it is away, and what direction it is coming from. When a dog doesn't bark you are unaware of where it is. It could be sitting right next to you and you never even know it.

Roof and the other gunmen who shot up churches, synagogues, schools, concerts, and night clubs, didn't just snap suddenly. No, they were calculating and strategic. They were able to move undetected while formulating and putting the pieces of their plans together.

After the ordeals were over and the investigation into their lives began it was discovered that they'd been plotting quietly in their rooms and on the internet, planning these horrific mass murders, for quite some time. I imagine Roof sat alone quietly in his room, for hours on end putting the pieces to his destructive and sinister plan together. His mother would probably check in on him occasionally, knocking on the door and asking him if everything is ok. He probably answered *'yes, Mom'*, and she went away. She knew something was wrong with him. Something wasn't quite right with him. Every mother has that intuition. But, since he never expressed his emotions or how he felt, she probably put it off as a phase in his life that he was going through.

Reports stated that Roof plotted and planned the Charleston massacre for six months without anyone noticing. Did his friends not recognize that something was wrong here? His parents had to have discerned some type of behavioral pattern changes but disregarded them. Maybe in retrospect they all looked back and saw the warning signs but a little too late. Many people attested that he typically kept to himself. One of his friends testified that Roof went on a racist rant about the return of segregation and white supremacy but no one took him serious. Friends and family were noted as saying that his unthinkable act of murdering those nine people came as a shock to everyone.

Unfortunately for the victims, *silence is the dark room where the devil develops his negatives* – and negatives are exactly what they are. *Evil grows in darkness.* It is on the canvas of the quiet mind that the devil paints his most vivid and colorful pictures. In the comfort of a quiet mind he can hide out and take his time, unbothered by outside distractions.

No one notices him building his diabolical plan in the mind of a quiet teenager who has shut out the world and retreated to solace. Alone in his bedroom with access to a world of evil directly through their cell phone or a computer.

There in the quietness he ponders and conjures up ways to get revenge on the world that refuses to see them or hear them. They are crying out inside to be heard and seen. Before long the quiet nerd, the reserved high school student, the socially awkward outcast, the anti-Semitic white supremacist disappears out of social interaction all together – until suddenly, reappearing with guns and bombs, shock and awe, brutally destroying the lives of innocent people. Unnoticed and undetected, the quiet devil was there all the while, formulating evil massacres in their minds. He was there hiding inside of a lie that he'd convinced them to accept as truth. Though they were quiet and peaceful on the outside, their thoughts were screaming violently on the inside of their minds. The loud silence is those raging emotions and evil thoughts that race wildly and shout loudly inside of the solitude of your mind that no one else can hear. *The quietest people have the loudest minds.*

THE DEVIL MADE ME DO IT

"God will not slap the forbidden fruit out of your hand."

As I mentioned in the beginning of this book, I realize that some people do not believe in devils. But that alone doesn't change their existence or make them any less real; no more than people who don't believe in gravity. A persons disbelief in gravity doesn't make them exempt from falling, nor does it change the truth about gravity.

And while some people choose not to believe in devils or demons, there are those of us who do believe. Among those of us who do believe, there is a distinctive line. The majority of those who do believe in devils, generally believe incorrectly. They have a warped and twisted perception of what devils really are. Many overly-spiritual and super-religious Christians believe that demons and devils have power to cross over from the supernatural realm into the natural realm and physically control people - making them do and say things absent of the person's permission. I don't subscribe to that notion. I choose to subscribe to a more comprehensible and spiritually-pragmatic idea. I believe that daily we all encounter and battle with devils more often than we realize. I believe that they are real but they can't physically touch humans. They have limited power in their ability to disturb natural things and physically interact with people, which I will explain in greater detail here in this chapter.

Some acknowledge the reality and existence of devils by saying things like *"we all have our own demons, or devils, to fight."* Some even choose to use specific titles to label the vices they are fighting with. For example, someone may refer to their vice or devil as alcoholism, pornography, a drug addiction, shop lifting, or gossiping.

However, the devil is none of these things, and none of these things are the devil. These vices are the manifestation of a tendency or temptation that a person can't control. The devil has influenced or convinced them to buy the lie that nothing is wrong with their addiction. He convinces them to believe that there addiction is not harming anyone else – that they can control their addiction. Or no real problem of overindulging in alcohol even exists. Mind you, the devil only has the power of suggestion. He can't physically touch you or force you to drink an alcoholic beverage; no more than he can physically force your mouth to curse and swear or force your hand to slap someone.

To better understand this point, let's identify and characterize what demons and devils really are and how they came to be. What are they and where did they come from? Demons and devils are spirits - evil spirits to be exact. They were originally created as angels, which are celestial beings that have celestial bodies. The celestial body of an angel gives them the ability to access both heaven and earth. Without a body, a spirit alone cannot gain access into the earth or physical realm. Demons and devils are the fallen angels that were kicked out of heaven with Lucifer. Lucifer was a high ranking angel who was kicked out of heaven for trying to lead a rebellion against God. Once Lucifer and the band of rebellious angels were kicked out of heaven, Lucifer became the devil, also known as satan. And the rebellious angels became demons, or little devils. Now, Satan and the other fallen angels are simply spirits without celestial bodies. They no longer have their celestial angelic bodies. They are in essence disembodied angels; just evil spirits.

The original Hebrew word for spirit means mental disposition or attitude. This is why people refer to someone who has a bad or negative attitude as someone who has a bad or evil spirit, and someone with a good attitude as someone who has a good spirit. This is also why people call liquor *spirits*, and uses the phrase *under the influence* to describe the effect liquor has on a person.

Liquor influences and alters a person's mind set and attitude. It influences a person to behave in a manner that is outside of the normal behavior of their sober mind. In like manner, evil spirits, demons have the ability to influence human beings; specifically their attitudes.

While the celestial body of an angel gives them the ability to access both heaven and earth, a spirit, be it good or evil, cannot access the physical realm without a body. Consequently, since devils and demons don't have bodies, they need the body of an earthly being to access and affect anything in the earth. This is why the devil needed to use the earthly body of a snake to gain access to deceive Eve and Adam. Otherwise, he could not have influenced them. Devils don't have bodies to operate in the earth, so they must use the power of suggestion and persuasion.

The devil has no real power other than suggestion and persuasion. Suggestion is the act of introducing or inducing a thought, sensation, or action in someone. Persuasion is the act of convincing someone to do or believe something. This usually happens through the sensory perceptions that lead to cravings and desires. If you see or smell a fresh baked cake as you are walking through the bakery section of a grocery store, your senses heighten and you want to taste it. You know you don't need it. You know that it is bad for your health. But you give in to the craving and desire to have a piece. You think it is your own thought so you help yourself to a piece. The devil suggests you eat more, and so you indulge. Afterwards, you feel guilty because you've eaten much more than you intended to eat.

The power of suggestion and persuasion can actually be stronger than the truth. Especially when you deny the truth or simply don't know the truth. For example, someone visits the doctor for an exam. The doctor tells the person that the test results show they are pre-diabetic. The doctor recommends that they exercise more and refrain from eating foods and drinking beverages that contain refined sugars. Yet, the person does not heed the truth, but chooses to believe the lie that they can, without consequence, continue eating the foods the doctor has forbidden. Inevitably, the prediabetes turns into type-2 diabetes because the person blatantly disregards the truth that the doctor has prescribed. Somewhere and somehow the person was persuaded, whether by an internal or external suggestion, that they were immune to the consequences of the doctor's truth. Or, maybe the person was wrongfully or ignorantly informed by someone else. Someone else who knows nothing about how to properly deal with diabetes.

Did the devil give the person diabetes? No.

Did the devil make the person eat the foods the doctor advised him not to eat? No.

The person alone bares the blame and responsibility for their actions and consequences. Could God have prevented the person from contracting diabetes? Yes.

Could God have stopped the person from eating the forbidden foods? Yes.

However, God will not slap the food out of you hand. Besides, God had already given the person the truth and they chose not to accept it or adhere to it. They simply did not want to take responsibility for their bad diet choices. So they attempt to shift the blame off of themselves onto the devil because it is easier to blame the devil rather than one's self.

For some people, *"the devil made me do it"* is an easy justification to pass off ones sins to someone or something else. It is an attempt to deny or deflect accountability for their own wrongdoings and wicked deeds. The devil may have suggested that you do it. But you are the one who did it. Many uninformed people of faith blame the devil for all the wrong they do, as well as the wrong that everyone else does. It's easy to shift the blame to the devil because the devil can't be seen. The devil can't be brought to trial. The devil can't be put in jail or punished by a court system. You can't hold the devil accountable for your wrong doings. So it is easy for a person to pass off their bad decisions and sinful behavior as the fault of the devil.

The devil doesn't "make" a husband cheat on his wife. The devil doesn't "make" a drug dealer sell drugs. The devil doesn't "make" a CEO steal millions of dollars from a company. The devil doesn't "make" a kidnapper, kidnap, a murderer murder, or a rapist rape. These are all self-initiated deeds driven by one's own selfish desires and tendencies.

I remember when we were children, in middle school, we played a game called "baddest man hit my hand". The initiator, usually a bully, would pick out two people. He would then stand in front of them, hold out his hands, and say to them both, "baddest man hit my hand". Once the person who considered himself the baddest man would hit the bullies extended hand, the bully would quickly say, "now hit that man"... referring to the other person. Almost ninety percent of the time, the baddest man would hit the other man, and a fight would soon follow. After the fight ended, there were often arguments and debates about who was to blame for starting the fight. Was it the bully who initiated the game, or the person who passed the first hit? Not an easy question to answer, depending on who you ask. Most would assume that the bully was to blame for starting the fight, when it was actually the person who passed the first blow. The bully did not take the persons hand and hit the other person. No.... he just used the game as a means to create a situation that lead to a fight. He used pride, shame and fear to influence one person to hit the other person.

The same thing happened in the garden with Adam and Eve when they ate from the forbidden tree. Adam blamed Eve, Eve blamed the serpent, and of course the devil blamed God. This is probably where the phrase, *"the devil made me do it"* derived from. When in all actuality, the devil hasn't "MADE" anyone do anything. The devil does not have the power to make anyone do anything. He simply suggests it. We are held responsible for the decisions and actions we make. You will not be able to blame the devil, when you have to give an account to God for the deeds you've done, whether good or bad.

The devil can't physically take your hand and make you eat the forbidden fruit, no more than God will slap the unforbidden fruit out of your hand to prevent you from eating it. God gives us the truth along with the power and strength to resist temptation. But He leaves the choosing to us.

Temptations are simply the suggestions and persuasions of the devil. When Eve was being deceived by the devil in the garden, the devil tempted her by suggesting that she eat the fruit from the forbidden tree. God could have supernaturally intervened and caused the wind to sway and swat the forbidden fruit out of Eve's hand, but He didn't. Or, even better, God could have just placed the tree on the outside of the garden where Adam and Eve could not get to it. But God placed the forbidden tree in the middle of the garden, where they had to walk by it every day.

Most people think It would be best if God removed their temptations all together, while some blame God for their weakness to temptation. They say things like *"God should not have placed the forbidden fruit around me, if He didn't want me to partake of it"*.

The people who say these things do not realize that avoiding temptation is not the answer to overcoming temptation. We don't grow spiritually by avoiding temptation or blaming God for our struggles with temptation. We build our spiritual strength by resisting temptation. A body builder tones his body by the resistance of weights. In like manner, men and women tone and develop their spiritual muscles and build their spiritual strength by resisting temptation.

It is very difficult to resist temptation when we are unarmed, in denial or ignorant of the truths about temptation. God gave Adam and Eve the truth about the trees in the garden. He told them which trees were permissible to eat from and which trees were forbidden to eat from. Armed with God's truth, they walked pass the forbidden tree every day and never touched their fruit. They didn't question God's truth and were never tempted to eat from the tree. It wasn't until the devil came along with his deceptive and contradicting suggestions and convinced them to go against the truth that they'd always adhered to.

As it relates to our health, God gives us the wisdom and knowledge of what to eat and what not to eat. He has provided his Word, doctors, and accessible information regarding what is acceptable and not acceptable to eat but the choice is ours. Sure, the devil will tempt you and suggest that you eat and drink things that are toxic and destructive to your body. But you are responsible for the actions. You will be judged and suffer the consequences for the things you ingest into your body, not the devil.

We must take full responsibility for the problems in our lives the same way that I did with fixing the leaking pipe. It's not always the devil's fault for things going wrong in our lives. Have you ever considered that what you are going through could be your fault? And more often than not, it is. The snake did not create the leak or the puddle. I created it. I created the problem by neglecting to address an issue that warranted my attention. Consequently, the mess attracted the snake. And getting rid of the devil does not solve the problem, no more than running the snake away does. Accepting accountability and fixing the mess are the first steps towards solving the problem.

The truth is this... the devil does not make you do anything. You do it on your own. He is just the influencer. However, you are the executer. He suggests it, but you put it into effect. The choice is yours, to do or not to do. To eat or not to eat. *God will not slap the forbidden fruit out of your hand.*

TERRY D. SWAIN

SECRET SINS

"What's done in the dark will come to the light."

There are a plethora of scriptures in the Bible that warn against covering up wrongdoings. Some of the scriptures even advise that evil deeds should be voluntarily confessed. That sounds really good in Church but not in reality. People are naturally conditioned to conceal their imperfections, weaknesses and less attractive behaviors. A convicted conscious prefers darkness rather than light. It is our instinctive reaction to hide when we are guilty. As children, we learned early how to lie to our parents and teachers to escape judgment. It is woven into the fabric of our very nature to hide them to avoid dealing with the consequences. When a child accidentally breaks their mothers' favorite coffee mug, without hesitation they immediately go into *"hide the evidence before anyone sees it"* mode. Even though it was an accident, they still feel the need to cover it up and keep it a secret instead facing the consequences head on.

This is the essence of where our struggle with telling the truth, acknowledging the truth, and standing in our truth derives from. We find ourselves wrestling with the decisions of what we should and should not conceal - on the basis of the consequences we may face. We get caught in a tug of war with truth and lies. Never realizing that when we question our convictions and morals it gives the quiet devil an invitation and opportunity to take advantage of our unwillingness to acknowledge the truth. In the words of Iyanla Vanzant, we must *'call a thing a thing'*, and *'stand in our truth'*. If you don't stand in your truth, you are avoiding the truth. And the truth will eventually catch up with you.

Numbers 32:23 says *'Be certain of this, your sins will catch up to you'*.

Such a simple and profound but often disregarded truth. And though it is simple to understand, we still try to hide and cover up our mistakes and weaknesses. Even from the beginning of time, humanity has attempted to hide its wrongdoings from God. Adam and Eve attempted to cover up their sin by clothing themselves with aprons made out of leaves, and then hiding out amongst the trees. They were attempting to hide from God by camouflaging themselves in with their environment.

The very first devil that Adam and Eve encountered in the earth was a quiet devil. He convinced them to eat the forbidden fruit and lie about eating it. And when the light of God's Presence came towards them, what did Adam and Eve do? They covered up and hid. And even though they covered their nakedness from each other, they were unable to cover themselves from God. After, they were found out and called forth to accountability, they started blame shifting. Adam blamed Eve, Eve blamed the devil, and of course the devil blamed God.

Ultimately, they received the consequences of their disobedience, which was eviction from their residence, their blessed place, the Garden of Eden. They were banned from the place that God had created specifically for them. A place that was perfectly created by God for them to thrive, excel and succeed in. But they messed that up. God even provided them the opportunity to come clean and confess their faults and they chose to stand behind the lie. They chose to trust in a lie instead of the truth.

Proverbs 28:13 says, *"whoever covers their sin will not prosper, but whosoever will confess and forsake their sin will have mercy."*

Covering up our sins never leads to prosperity. Even if it seems that we have gotten away, we still have the defeat of a guilt-ridden conscious. Adam and Eve could have leveled with God and received grace and forgiveness. If they had only come forward and been honest about what happened they would have found mercy immediately.

In the book of **Judges 16**, there is a story about Samson and Delilah. It is a twisted love story of lust, lies and betrayal. Samson's love interest Delilah secretly cohorts with his enemies, the Gazites, who were relentless in their attempts to discover the secret sauce to his strength. They wanted to use his weakness to capture him. So they bribed Delilah, each offering her 1100 pieces of silver for the secret to his strength. Samson revealed his secret to her one night while resting his head in her lap. He was at his most vulnerable state.

When a man lays his head in a woman's lap, he has already laid his heart in her hand.

As she was caressing his face and stroking his ego he revealed to her that the source of his strength was the locks of his hair.

His enemies, now armed with this information, made several attempts to capture Samson. On one particular covert operation to catch him, they were lying in wait outside of Delilah's house. They waited quietly all night hiding in the darkness. They determined that in the morning when it was day, they were going to kill him. Much like Samson's enemies, the Gazites, the quiet devil hides in the darkness waiting for the perfect opportunity to overthrow its victim. He uses the elements of patience and surprise. The reason the quiet devil is the most dangerous of all devils is because he can hide out in the silence of darkness. His quietness allows him to go undetected.

He can't remain in a place where light and truth are because he will be exposed. He can only dwell in lies. When we lie to each other and when we lie to ourselves, we are blocking out the light of the truth from shining in. We intentionally and consciously create a space in our hearts where we are harboring the quiet devil. He becomes a permitted fugitive in our minds, allowed to

Samson gave his enemies an invitation to ambush him when he put his trust in a woman who wasn't God's choice for him. He loved her but she didn't love him.

In the end, she proved herself to be no good for him. If he would have stopped entertaining and pursuing her, he would have never been in the position to be ambushed. Samson deceived himself into thinking that he was the exception to the rule. He thought that the rules applied to everyone else but himself. He thought that he could play with sin and temptation and not get harmed by it. He thought that he could be disobedient and still avoid the consequences. He kept going back through a door that God had shut. A door that he was never meant to go through. A woman he was never supposed to be involved with.

God will shut the doors that we are not supposed to go through, but He will not lock them.

On several occasions God shut the door to Delilah by allowing circumstances between him and Delilah to go unfavorable on numerous occasions. Unfortunate things happened whenever Samson had any interactions with Delilah. These unfortunate set of events happened to warn and also inform Samson that she was not the woman for him. Yet, Samson disregarded, persisted and pushed through all of the warning signs and kept opening the door that God had shut.

Much like many of us, we wear down the edges of our convictions and beliefs when we continue to secretly indulge in what is off limits to us. We intentionally push past the obvious and clear warning signs, disregarding the signs over and over again. Until, the points on our conscious wear down so far that there is no edge remaining to slow us down from spiraling into sin. Like brake pads on a car or the spokes on a bicycles chain ring. They both are designed to slow you down when you apply the brakes. Over time they will wear dull to the point that they are no longer able to perform the function they were created for – to stop the vehicle or bicycle.

Consequently, when our conscious no longer stop us from going down the wrong path or choosing the wrong things, it places us in a reprobated mind state... breezing through the stop signs and red lights of our convictions, like an out of control car with no brakes. Eventually, veering over the limits and crashing. Damaging our lives and others lives in the process.

Many people, just like Samson, are deceived into thinking that they are invincible to sin. Deceived into believing that they are smart enough to get away and escape the consequences. No matter how careful you are you will eventually get caught.

There is a reason why boundary lines and speed limits are placed along the roads. They set limits and restrictions. They are there as visual aids to help us travel safely without harming ourselves or others. If, and when, you veer too far over the boundary lines, you can crash and harm yourself as well as others. God's Word and our convictions serve the same purpose as the boundary lines and speed limits along the highways. They keep us safely on the right path, as long as we obey and heed them. This is why it is so important that we set and settle personal convictions in all aspects of our life, based on truth. Whenever we refuse to set and settle our convictions, we have no marker to gauge or determine how far is too far.

In the case of Samson, he veered too far over the lines of caution and wrecked his life terribly. So bad that he never recovered from it. He refused to turn on the light of truth. Due to his blatant disobedience and disregard for his personal convictions, his enemies were successful at capturing him, cutting his hair off, robbing him of his secret God-given strength, and blinding him. They took his vision and left his life in utter darkness, literally.

Samson continued to sneak around in the darkness with Delilah, even after she repeatedly showed him that she did not have his best interest at heart. He never imagined that she would cause so much damage to his life. We too, like Samson, damage our lives severely whenever we play and stay too long in the darkness of hidden and covered sin.

John 3:10-21 says, *"People choose to walk in the darkness by keeping secrets and telling lies, when their actions are evil. Everyone* *who practices doing wrong hates the light, neither do they come into the light, unless their wrong doings will be exposed. But the people who practice doing what is right come to the light, so their actions may be exposed, to ensure that they are doing what is right in the sight of God.*

Those who intentionally do wrong and cover up their actions are refusing to come into the light. No robber, thief, murderer, rapist or criminal prefers to commit crimes in the day time. They'd rather wait and commit crimes in the night when it's dark. When it is quiet and less people are awake. The same goes for anyone who has something to hide. Darkness conceals contemptable actions and light reveals contemptable actions. Police have even discovered that when interrogating criminal suspects, they are more prone to tell the truth when they are in rooms that are well lit, rather than rooms that have dim lighting. This is why it is important for people who truly want to escape the prison of guilt and shame to confess their actions and come clean. Standing in the light of truth brings freedom. Some people do not truly want to be liberated from their lies, lust and wrongful behavior. So they will forever remain in darkness until their lies or secrets are inevitably exposed. *What's done in the dark will eventually come to the light.*

NAKED AND NOT ASHAMED

"A lie is the devil's favorite hiding place."

The devil has an arsenal of vices and tactics that he can use to gain access into a person's mind and their life. He uses secrets, youthful lusts, doubt, ignorance, religion, self-righteousness, excuses, justified sins, half-truths, exaggerations, pride, and arrogance, to name a few. All of these things create a dark space within a person's mind that the devil can hide out in. But, out of all his deceptive tactics, *the devil's favorite hiding place is a lie*. A lie is the devil's greatest and most effective weapon. Lies give the devil permission, opportunity, and direct access to meddle in a person's mind and life. Once he gains that access he hides out in that dark space, and there he builds his stronghold.

The reason he prefers to use a lie is because he knows that people will go to relentless extremes to protect a lie. Never realizing that while they are protecting their lie from being exposed, they are also protecting the quiet devil who's hiding inside of their lie.

Every sin begins with a lie. If you trace any sin that you have ever committed back to its root, it will always lead you to a lie. And every lie, if not confessed, will inevitably lead you to pain, shame and destruction.

In the beginning, Adam and Eve did not wear clothing because they were unashamed. There was no shame or vulgarity associated with being naked. They could look upon each other with innocence like a child, not once ever viewing nakedness as something dirty or indecent. It wasn't until after the devil convinced them to believe a lie, which lead them to sin, that all changed. Once they ate from the forbidden tree, their eyes were open to the evil nature of sin. They now looked upon one another with shame and obscenity. They immediately made clothing from the leaves to cover their nudity along with their shame and guilt. All because of a lie. Lies bring shame and disgrace but truth brings honor and virtue.

There are stages to sin and lying is the first stage.

James 1:15 says, *when lust has conceived, it brings forth sin: and sin, when it is finished, brings forth death.*

Lust is temptation. It is simply a lie covered in sugar, spice and everything nice. It is whatever your sweet tooth weakness is. It is a lie wrapped up inside of your desires and fantasies. And once you bite into it, you immediately realize that it was not what it appeared to be. It turns out to be poison instead of pleasure. Sour instead of sweet. Hurtful instead of helpful.

The old bait and switch trick. The old carrot on a shoe string trick. The devil doesn't have any new tricks. He just has the old recycled and remixed versions of the same old tricks that he has always used since the beginning of time. It's all a trap. He lures you in by your fleshly desires and imprisons you.

He doesn't enslave a person straightaway. No, that's too much work. There is a process and strategy. There are stages and levels to getting you trapped in the grip of an addiction, an affair or an immoral lifestyle.

First, he deceives and convinces you to *buy the lie*. The lie that it is ok to do wrong, it's ok to give in to your sinful tendencies; especially if it serves your own selfish desires. Secondly, after you buy the lie, you *do the deed* - indulging in the act of sinful pleasure. And lastly, after you do the deed, you *develop an appetite*, and you are now hooked. You are now entangled in bondage. You are now addicted to the taste of the sin that all began with a lie.

It was a lie that convinced me to smoke weed for the first time.

Unlike most of my peers, I escaped high school without experimenting with drugs. I dibbled and dabbled with alcohol but I never smoked weed, popped pills or used any other drugs. It was after I moved away and went to college that I was enticed and gave in to the peer pressure to smoke marijuana. I was room mating with my cousin who'd been smoking for several years. He smoked nearly every day. He'd wake and bake. Every morning he'd wake up and roll up a couple of joints; one to smoke before school, one to smoke after school, and one to smoke before the day ended.

From time to time he would ask if I wanted to smoke with him and I'd always decline his offer. Until one day, after leaving school, we went to kickback at a local Park and hang out. We were sitting on the car listening to music and my cousin pulled out a fat bag of that sticky.

Well, it wasn't a fat bag nor was it sticky. We didn't even know about sticky weed or any other strand for that matter. It was actually a bag of what we later termed "dirt weed". It was weed that he'd stolen from his father's personal homegrown stash. It was always full of stems and seeds, which made the joint or blunt pop and burst open whenever the fire burnt across one of the stems or seeds. To be perfectly honest, the weed would barely get us high. We'd have to smoke several oversized blunts before we could even feel the full effect of the weed kicking in. I remember nights when we'd blow through six or seven blunts just to maintain a semi-high throughout the night. Anyway, that was me drifting and reminiscing. Let's get back to the original point that I was making.

So, we were at the park chilling and he fired up a joint and started smoking it. He asked if I wanted to hit it and I declined his offer the first time. He continued to assert that weed is harmless. It just makes you laugh and gives you the munchies.

After several minutes of debating, I finally gave in to the peer pressure and my curiosity got the best of me. I bought into the lie. I took a hit of the joint and after about five minutes I felt the high kicking in. And... just as he'd said, I began laughing sporadically and contagiously at almost everything. I was slowly and gradually pulled in to a state of euphoria. I bought the lie and did the deed.

Sin always begins with a lie. I accepted my cousins position that weed only makes you laugh and gives you the munchies. When in reality, weed does much more than just make you laugh and hungry. From that day forward I began to indulge more and more and started smoking weed on a regular basis, almost daily.

Years after that first hit, I battled with the negative effects of smoking weed. He didn't tell me that I would lose out on opportunities because my urine was tested positive for marijuana. I lost out on job opportunities because I failed drug screenings. I also lost out on music opportunities because I was high at meetings and recording sessions. He didn't tell me about the long-term problems I'd experience like trouble thinking clearly, not being able to organize my thoughts, trouble multitasking and trouble remembering things.

I discovered that sustained marijuana use can also slow down your reaction time, it was proven to increase high school dropout probability among younger users, and could also produce respiratory problems such as bronchitis and lung cancer.

I was unaware that with that first toke of marijuana, I'd just given the quiet devil permission to start building his stronghold based on the lie that I'd accepted. No one tells you the ugly truth about the dangers of indulging in the pleasures of fleshly desires. My cousin only sold me the sweet exterior of temptation. He coated the lie with sweet pleasures. He did not share with me any of the ugly and bitter troubles that are associated with smoking weed. Now that the lie had been accepted and the deed had been done, the only thing left for the quiet devil to do was influence me to develop an appetite, which he did. I'd now developed the appetite which is the grip of any addiction, tendency or behavior. The appetite is the addictive taste and hunger to continue using or indulging in harmful behaviors. With each use, with each indulgence, the appetite grew and the grip tightened. It wasn't sudden. It was subtle. It all began with a lie. The same lie that the devil used in the beginning, in the Garden of Eden, with Adam and Eve.

Peoples attempt to compromise and justify their wrongdoings and misbehavior is another reason why the devils' favorite hiding place is a lie. One of the most commonly used appropriations for compromising and justifying wrongdoings is secrets. He convinces people to believe that secrets are not the same as lies, when they are in fact the same. *A secret is just a well-covered lie.* It is a lie that's buried alive. It is the withholding and hiding of the truth and facts. A secret is a lie that just hasn't been discovered or uncovered yet. The deception of the devil is to make a person believe that a lie is dead because it is concealed. But, everything buried is not dead. A lie continues to live beneath the deceptive covering of a secret. Since keeping secrets is concealing the truth and withholding information, it can actually be considered theft by deception, because a person who lies or keeps secrets from someone is stealing that person's trust without their consent.

A secret and a lie are both tools used to control and manipulate. People lie to control the outcome of a situation for their own benefit, favor or advantage. If I keep a secret about something I've done wrong, then I am attempting to escape the negative consequences and continue enjoying the immoral pleasures that I am lying to protect. The quiet devil hides behind this manipulative way of thinking and he will continue to hide there while establishing his stronghold, until you disturb him. Until you expose him by telling the truth. If the quiet devil is never confronted or exposed he will continue to keep you in the same cycle of bondage.

Be warned, he will take you further than you want to go, keep you longer than you want to stay, and cost you more than you are willing to spend.

The pleasures of sin are only for a season, according to **Hebrews 11:25**.

The pleasures of sin are temporary. So once the season of sins pleasure comes to an end, the quiet devil will have killed, stolen and destroyed everything that God has spent years building in your life.

If truth and light are not occupying those disengaged, vacant and dark spaces within us that we are passive about, then that space is susceptible and accessible to the devil for habitation. That space becomes a place that the devil can utilize as his hiding place to set up his blockade. I in the same manner that the Gazite men setup Samson did when they captured him. Once the blockade of the devil's strong hold is erected in your mind, it prevents you from escaping. Even when you come to the point that you want to get out of the mess you've allowed yourself to get stuck in, the grip of the stronghold will stop you. The Gazites surrounded Samson and positioned themselves to besiege him. They waited quietly all night at the exits and entrances to obstruct any possible passages of escape. The entire time they were setting up their ambush, Samson was unaware because he was blinded by his lust for Delilah. His enemies did not speak or move until the opportunity arrived for them to seize and kill him. The element of surprise is best rendered when a person least expects it. This is why the devil positions his self and waits quietly and carefully in his place until the best time to attack is presented. The same tactic he used with the gunmen in all of the mass shootings. No one ever saw any of the attacks coming until they happened. He will attack our lives in the same manner, if we don't expose him first and denounce the lie he is hiding in.

The quiet devil is sure to take his time and establish a firm strong hold first before attacking. For this cause, he will lay dormant for extensive amounts of time, even years, waiting for the perfect and most effective and vulnerable moment to destroy your life. He hides in the recesses of a lustful tendency, and slowly develops an atrocious addiction.

Take pornography for example. It can begin with an innocent scroll down your social media time line. As you are scrolling, you come across a video post of a woman who captures your attention. She is dressed provocative or dancing seductively and appeals to your particular taste and desire. The build of her body, the curves in her figure, or the way she moves begins to arouse and provoke sexual fantasies within your mind. You begin to imagine yourself engaging in sexual relations with her. You are enjoying what you see, so you decide to entertain your fantasies a bit more by replaying the seductive video several more times. You indulge in this erotic pleasure for a while until you finally break away. You close out of that particular video and continue scrolling down your timeline. You like a few posts, respond to some comments and then log off for the day. The seed is now planted and you can't wait to get alone again to watch more. Over time the lust increases and the desire to watch porn begins to take over your life. You lie and tell yourself that you are not addicted, you just enjoy watching porn. You tell yourself it is harmless, but the appetite has now developed. It begins to negatively affect your relationships and your daily productivity. You're now watching porn on your laptop when you are at home, on your phone while you are driving and even on your work computer during office hours.

The stronghold is set and the addiction has set in. The quiet devil is now at work in your life, in your mind and in your desires. He is working to destroy your convictions and your consciousness toward lust. You continue to disregard the negative impact it is having on your life and you refuse to denounce the lie. And he remains quietly seated in the darkness of that lie building his strategy and stronghold. *A lie is the devil's favorite hiding place.*

TERRY D. SWAIN

BREAKING THE GRIP

"Take off the muddy boots, before you start mopping the floor."

If you are ever going to truly break free from the grip of the quiet devil, you have to put your foot down and stop giving in to his temptation. You have to take total control over your situation and break free. In martial arts defensive training they teach that the most effective way to get free from an arm grip, also known as a sleeve grip, is to lift your knee up to the assailants wrist and push against it while simultaneously pulling your arm away. Eventually the grip will break. It happens almost immediately. It's so effective that it really doesn't matter the size of the assaulter. 100 pound females have used it to break free from 200 plus pound males. The method is a bit unorthodox but it works. It's only by taking matters into your hand and being willing to do whatever it takes to get free will you be able to escape the grip of the quiet devil's hold.

Many people say they want to be free from addictions, tendencies, affairs, and habits but they are not willing to do what is required to be free. True freedom requires changed behavior. It requires challenging habitual behaviors. You can't keep doing the same thing that got you in trouble and expect to get out of it. *You can never clean a floor by mopping it in muddy boots.* You have to take the muddy boats off first... before you start mopping the floor. Before you can clean up a mess you have to stop what's causing the mess. If you don't identify the root cause, you will be forever fighting a losing battle and working against yourself. If you keep on the muddy boots, you will keep tracking dirt and mud back into the same areas you just cleaned up. This is why many people are caught in a never ending cycle of dealing with the same ole drama, the same type of men, the same financial problems and the same type of addictions. It may show up at a different time, a different place, with a different face and name, but it is the same thing.

You will never see progress from your efforts, until you recognize that you are the one who is causing the problem.

The first thing you have to do is remove the muddy boots. Then mop up the mess. Stop repeating the same destructive patterns.

In order for you to clean up the mess you've created in your own personal life, whether it is an emotional, relational, financial, health related, or any other type of mess, you have to see it as a problem. You have to change the motivation behind why you want to clean it up. Why do you want to be delivered from the addiction? Why do you want to be free from the bad habit? Why do you want to be loosed from the affair? Why do you want to end an unhealthy relationship?

It is not a chore to do something that you want to do. It is not grievous and resentful to remove something or someone from your life when you are doing it for the right reasons. It is only a chore and difficult to detach from it when you are not yet convinced that it is a real problem. If not, you will eventually get comfortable living in the mess and normalize it, when it is not normal to live in a chaotic and unhealthy state. Until the lesson is learned you will keep repeating it, because *a lesson not learned is a lesson repeated.*

This is exactly why it is called a stronghold and not weak hold. It is difficult to break free from something that has a strong grip on you. The word "stronghold" derives from 16th century vocabulary. A stronghold was a fortified wall built around a castle to defend and protect it from attack. The context of the word is still the same today, carrying the idea of holding something securely. This is absolutely the case when it comes to negative ties with things and people that are difficult to break free from. They fortify your life with lies, secrets, guilt, shame and sin to block you in from the truth that desires to liberate you. Hiding in the darkness, behind the fortified walls of every sinful tendency, bad habit and destructive addiction is the quiet devil. And the walls of his strong holds are built by those very lies, secrets, and deceit that lured you in.

It was not an easy task for armies to break through the fortified walls of a castle or city, but it wasn't impossible. It just took a strategic approach, the right weaponry and a relentless will to overcome.

Defeating the quiet devil and destroying his stronghold is a battle, much like any military battle. Yet, it is not a physical battle because the devil is not a physical enemy.

Devils are spirits. They are spiritual beings. You are fighting a spiritual enemy and a spiritual battle. The battle is psychological. It is not fought with your body, it is fought with your mind. You can't beat a spiritual enemy using physical weapons like guns, swords and grenades. Neither can you defeat a spiritual enemy with tears, bickering, complaining or profanity. Those are all natural, emotional and physical weapons that can never prevail against a spiritual foe. You can't cry your way out of an addiction. You can't complain your way out of a poverty mindset. You can't cuss and swear your way out of depression. It just doesn't work like that.

The devil doesn't respond to your emotions, crying and bickering. He responds to spiritual things. To defeat a spiritual enemy, you must use spiritual weapons such as prayer, faith, truth, wisdom, the Word of God, obedience and will power. These are the weapons of our spiritual warfare. **2 Corinthians 10:3-4** shares this same insight, which says:

"For though we walk in the flesh, we do not war after the flesh. For the weapons of our warfare are not physical, but mighty through God to the pulling down of strong holds".

We are not strong enough to break free from addictions, habits and tendencies in our own physical strength. We have to use the spiritual weapons that God has made available to us. Spiritual weapons produce the power, grace and anointing that is needed to break the grip of the devil's stronghold. **Isaiah 10:27** gives us some more insight into what a stronghold is and how it works,

"And it shall come to pass in that day, that his burden shall be taken away from off your shoulder, and his yoke from off your neck, and the yoke shall be destroyed because of the anointing".

A yoke, in Old Testament biblical times, was a wooden device that farmers used on their oxen when plowing fields. The yoke clasped around the neck of two oxen, binding them together. The yoke fit around the neck of the oxen like handcuffs and were used to control the direction and speed of the oxen as they pulled the plow through the fields. The farmer used the reigns that were attached to the yoke, to control the oxen, in the same manner that an owner controls a dog on a leash or a cowboy controls a horse with a bridle. Looking at this same principle from a spiritual perspective, we can see how the quiet devil uses the stronghold like a yoke, to control the people who are entrapped or bound by his lies, secrets and deceit.

A man or woman can develop a soul tie, also considered a stronghold, through a sexual affair. And even when they want to end the affair, it is difficult do so because they are still connected spiritually or soulishly. By the way, you won't find *"soulishly"* in the dictionary because I just made that word up. It means *of or relating to the human soul.* A soul tie is the invisible connection that binds two people together through the act of sex. And like the yoke the farmer uses to direct the ox, a soul tie can control another person.

Like the strings on a puppet, one lover can pull the soul tie strings of the other person in the affair because they have something over their head to use as leverage. No pun intended. The leverage they have over the other lover is the threat of exposing their secret dirty deeds. So, every time the other person wants to walk away from the affair, the other person pulls on the invisible leash. The quiet devil does the same thing. Except he uses his leverage to pull the strings on the inside of your mind. He uses the strings connected to your guilty conscious.

Many people try to walk away from addictions, affairs and lustful tendencies but are often unsuccessful, simply because the pull and grip is too deep and too strong for them to break away from it in their own strength. It requires a spiritual remedy called *the anointing* to break free. The anointing has the ability to release a person from the grip of the devil's entrapment.

The anointing is compared to oil; specifically olive oil. Olive oil can be used as a lubricant that makes an object slippery. It gives an object the ability to slip away or escape. For example, if you grip a person's dry arm, it is difficult and nearly impossible for them to pull away. But, once the oil is applied to the persons arm, they are able to pull away easily and almost immediately. Whenever you denounce and stop believing the lies that got you into bondage to begin with, you are applying the oil of the anointing. When you are not using the right tools, weapons, principles and tactics to get free, it is always difficult to pull away. As stated earlier in the martial arts example, you must push and pull simultaneously, to break free. Force must be applied to escape the grip of bondage. You have to forcefully push harmful things and people away, while simultaneously pulling yourself away from them. The anointing gives you the ability to pull away. It is an added spiritual agent that assists you and gives you the extra edge or advantage needed to overcome. The anointing is not some spooky spiritual power floating from Heaven. It is the power that is released from the proper application of wisdom, knowledge and understanding. When it is applied properly to your circumstances, it produces the anointing, or power, needed to change your circumstances. This is why you can be bound by cigarettes, drugs or alcohol for years and are never able to break free. This is why you can be entrapped in a scandal, affair or racket for years and are never able to cut ties. This is why you can be battling with depression, guilt or anxiety for years and are never able to overcome; even after numerous attempts to stop indulging. The reason why you have not been able to break free, cut ties and overcome is you don 't have, or have not properly applied the wisdom and knowledge to change your situation.

The same applies to the mopping scenario. Mopping requires pushing and pulling. Your will and desire to be free is the pushing motion. Your will gives you the strength to *push* away from your negative circumstances. But it is the wisdom and knowledge that gives you the power to *pull* away from your circumstances.

In order to get the floor clean when mopping, you have to push and pull until the floor is clean.

Until you are clean, metaphorically.

Clean is a term used to describe the condition of people who are free from, or no longer bound by an addiction. Therefore, to get clean from an addiction, a negative relationship, depression, lustful tendencies, criminal behavior, bad habits, a grudge or anything that has a stronghold on you, it requires changed behavior. It requires your efforts and commitment to pushing and pulling the mop of changed behavior, over the floor of your mind until it is clean. Until it is free from the grip of the quiet devil. *Take off the muddy shoes, before you start mopping the floor.*

EVICTION NOTICE

"When you kick the devil out, be sure to change the locks."

A wise man said, *"Don't let people rent space in your head, if they don't pay rent"*. If you don't pay, you can't stay. It's simple as that. If a tenant refuses to pay rent to their landlord, or leave voluntarily, then at some point they will be evicted. The tenant and the tenant's belongings will be removed from the residence. The same goes for your mental space. If anyone or anything is taking up space in your mind without permission or admission, they have to go. *You are the landlord of your mind*. You are responsible for evicting any and every thought that is not paying rent or adding value to your mind space.

Your mind is a space for creative and purposeful use. Your mind space is valuable and how you allow it to be occupied is critical to your peace, sanity and prosperity. You should not worry yourself or give much thought to the opinions of other people who do not add value to your life. If you give your mind to things that don't matter, or shouldn't matter, then you are wasting precious time that can be used for the things that do matter. The things that contribute to your welfare and add value to your life. Never allow things or people to cloud your mind space with stress, worry, anxiety, depression, guilt, condemnation, or regret. You have the power to evict them.

The quiet devil uses the clutter of unhealthy thoughts to rent out space in your head. This is why we must guard the entrance to our mind, spirit and emotions from brain garbage. *Brain garbage is anything that adds no purposeful value to your life*. Like junk food to your body. It has no nutritional value. Brain garbage is gossip, negative news, trashy reality shows, senseless social media content, and vanity music. You have to protect your spirit and rid your mind of brain garbage. Like an unlawful tenant, who enters your property illegally, you must serve them an eviction notice. You have to cast them out. And after the eviction has been served, the locks need to be changed also. Changing the locks on a home is the same as changing your mindset and behavior. If your mindset and behavior is never changed, you run the risk of the same issue returning again. Changing your mindset and behavior is the restoration process. Once you break free and get clean from any type of stronghold, you must allow God to help you restore your mind. In the same manner that a landlord has to restore their property back to good condition, after a tenant has been evicted. You too must restore your mind space. You must put in the work to rehab your mind.

Earlier in the book we compared the quiet devil to a squatter. A squatter being a person who takes up residence in a home that belongs to someone else, while cunningly attempting to take possession of the home as their own. Whenever you cast out (*evict*) a devil, you remove the devil from the premises. Removing him makes it possible for the rightful owner to regain ownership of their mind space and their life again. On one occasion in the Bible, Jesus met a demon possessed man who was living in the graveyard. HE was living there because the demons were tormenting him mentally. The Bible accounts that the demon possessed man was *"not in his right mind"*. This implies that the man was "OUT" of his mind. He was not at home, mentally or psychologically.

He was not behind the steering wheel of his thoughts.

He was not in control of his mind.

He was being influenced by something else.

When Jesus cast out the demon, the man was able to regain control of his mind and his thoughts. Afterwards, Jesus sat and taught the man, restoring his mind and removing any point of reference for the demon to return to. In a sense, Jesus changed the locks. If the devil attempted to return, his key would no longer work.

The key represents the point of reference. As long as people hold the key to access your life, they will continue to return. But when the locks are changed, he may still return with the old key and insert it into the key hole. However, old keys don't work in new locks. So the key may fit, but it no longer turns the lock.

Old ways don't work on new mindsets.

The devils old tricks no longer work on a new attitude.

The abusive partners words no longer work on a new way of thinking.

This is why you have to stop giving the devil and abusive people the keys to access your life. You have to stop giving them points of reference.

Like the snake in the water puddle story. The leak was the point of reference. The leak created the puddle that kept the snake returning. It is the point of reference that keeps people returning to unhealthy choices, destructive situations, bad habits and sinful temptations. Issues in your life will always resurface when they have a point of reference to connect back to.

You must remove the point of references.

You must close the doors.

You must change the locks.

Change the thoughts and behaviors. Lock out the lies, the evil thoughts, and the impure motives that give the quiet devil access back into your life.

What is the point of reference that keeps allowing depression to creep back into your life?

What have you allowed to remain as a reference point for the quiet devil to return to?

What thing are you holding on to that connects you to that destructive addiction?

What are you holding on to that connects you back to that unhealthy relationship?

You have to cut the ties that bind. The grip of sin can only remain when the doorway to access your life is still open or unlocked. Whenever we hold on to secret memoirs of sin, we not only leave the door open and unlocked, but we leave the key under the mat for the quiet devil – giving him access to come in and out of our lives as he pleases, whenever he wants to.

If we do not remove those secret points of references out of our lives, we are leaving a dark space for the devil to hide out in. Points of reference can be a phone number of an ex-lover saved in your phone under a secret name. It can be the dime bag of cocaine secretly hid away in the shoe box in the back of your closet. It can be a line of communication left open to an unhealthy relationship. It could be memorabilia from something or someone that triggers and rekindles the memories of old habits and behaviors. A point of reference can be a number of things that you have shut out but you haven't locked the door on. By not cutting the tie or locking the door, there remains an opportunity or chance for the bondage to return.

Flames that are not put out correctly and completely can be rekindled. The right gust of wind can reignite the fire. The quiet devil knows how to blow on the kindles of hidden and unresolved feelings to reignite old flames. He is good at hiding beneath the surface of smoldering ashes, waiting in silence for the perfect opportunity to fan the flames and ignite the same fire that burnt you and hurt others before.

We can only, truly, sever the tie and break the grip of the quiet devil when we choose to denounce the lie we have accepted as truth and dispose of every remaining point of reference that attracts him. This only happens when we get sick and tired of dealing with the same detrimental issues and finally lock the devil out once and for all.

When I realized the puddle was attracting the snake and could potentially attract other deadly snakes to my home, and could potentially harm me or my family, I had to do something about it. I had to do something quick to fix the problem. I had to go above and beyond the usual methods that I had previously applied. I solicited the help of someone who knew more about fixing leaking pipes than I did. I solicited the help and advice of a professional. Whenever we are unable to resolve issues on our own, with our limited knowledge, experience and strength, then we must call on someone who is more experienced and qualified. Someone who has the authority and wisdom to do what we haven't been able to do. We must seek help from the all-knowing, all-wise and all-powerful God! He not only has the know-how to fix our problems, but He has also placed other people in the earth who He has given the knowledge, skill and expertise to help us. We must know when to lean on and reach out to the Mentors, Coaches and Wise men that God has purposefully placed in our lives for such times as these.

When I was finally convinced and persuaded that something had to be done, I took assertive actions to fix the leak. The right way. I dug up the ground around the leaking pipes and took pictures of the damaged fittings and broken pipes. Next, I headed to the hardware store. I showed the pictures of the faulty pipes to the store owner and he was able to help me find everything I needed to repair the waterline. He talked me through each step to repair the pipes and also gave me some helpful tips.

He did not come to my house and fix the pipes for me or with me. He simply gave me the knowledge and instructions and sold me the tools I needed to fix it myself. God is like the hardware store owner. He gives us everything we need to fix the problems in our lives because He wants us to fix them ourselves. When other people fix our problems for us, we have to call on them again when things fail or come apart. But, if we fix them ourselves, we gain the knowledge and experience to repair them. Not only can we fix it again, but we can pass that knowledge on to others who are dealing with the same or a similar issue. We have the ability to empower others with the knowledge we have acquired from our experiences. Sometimes we go through to get something out of it for ourselves. Then there are times when we go through things to get something out of it for someone else.

I worked tirelessly replacing the pipes until I finally fixed the leak. After the leak was properly fixed, the water puddle eventually receded and the snake never returned. I broke the grip of the quiet devil's stronghold and left him with nothing to return to. I am sure the snake occasionally slithered back looking for the puddle that he'd once enjoyed, only to realize that it no longer existed. In the same way, people and things that once had free access to your life through the lustful pleasures of sin will come back looking for that same place to return to. But they will not be able to get in because the key no longer works. *"When you kick the devil out, be sure to change the locks."*

IN CONCLUSION

As long as there is something to return to, the quiet devil will return. But, if there is nothing in you for him to return to, he will eventually give up and go away. When you resist the devil he will flee. Where there is no wood, the fire goes out. Temptation is like fire. It can only burn with fuel. Stop putting logs on the fire and it will eventually burn out. This is why it is imperative to get rid of everything and everyone that attracts the same old pain, temptation and problems back into your life. Nothing is worth your freedom, your peace or your sanity. As the landlord of your mind and spirit, you MUST make it a priority to seal off every access point into your life. Change your thoughts and behaviors, and even your phone number if necessary.

My question to you now is this.

How bad do you want to be free and untangled from the trappings of the quiet devils stronghold?

Are you willing to give up your lustful tendencies and change your behaviors?

Are you willing to fight for your freedom?

Are you willing to let go of everything and everyone that is not good for you?

Are you willing to make the difficult sacrifices to break free from fleshly and selfish desires?

You have to be real with yourself and answer these questions truthfully. Because as long as you are still undecided or halfway in and halfway out, then you are only deceiving yourself. You are also deceiving your family and loved ones. The people who are connected to you by covenant relationship. Covenant relationships are the relationships that hold great value to you. Relationships that you are connected to by promises, vows or commitments. Relationships like your parents, your spouse, your children or significant other. The relationships that you hold dear to that must be protected at all costs. These are the relationships that can be easily hurt, damaged or destroyed by betrayal, deception, lies and disloyalty.

Understand that your decisions don't just effect you. They directly and indirectly impact the lives of those you love. Those who are close to you. And you owe it to yourself and them to break free and remain free.

Freedom belongs to you.

It is yours.

It is not some fleeting illusion that can never be obtained.

It is right in front of you. Closer than you think. Close enough for you to reach out and lay hold on it.

Now that I have provided you with the tools that you need to break free and remain free, the rest is up to you. I have done my part. Now you must do your part. I've led you to the water. Now you have to drink from the fountain of life.

Today I have set before you cursing and blessing, bondage and freedom, death and life.

Choose life!

Choose to overcome!

Choose to go to work rebuilding the life you lost! Recover the life you were always meant to live and deserve to live. Redeem the times. Restore and mend the relationships that were damaged and the friendships that were destroyed by the quiet devil. It's time to come out of the silent darkness into the marvelous light.

You are no longer bound!

You are no longer defeated!

You are free!

You are triumphant!

You are victorious!

TERRY D. SWAIN

This book was written for informational purposes only. To the end that some or all of the information contained within it is able to adequately inform and equip the reader with knowledge and wisdom to make the first step towards your specific path towards freedom, recovery and healing.

The contents of this book is not intended to be a substitute for professional spiritual, mental or medical advice, diagnosis, or treatment. Always seek the advice of a physician or other qualified professional with any questions you may have regarding a medical, spiritual or psychological condition. Never disregard professional medical advice or therapy, or delay in seeking it because of something you have read in this book.

If you think you may need spiritual, mental or psychiatric assistance, reach out to a licensed and trusted physician, therapist or counselor. If you feel that your condition is an emergency, call your doctor, go to the emergency department, or call 911 immediately.

A great place to begin your search for a qualified mental health professional is to seek the advice of your primary care physician who likely has plenty of local mental health colleagues. Early help for a mental health issue can make a huge difference.

When you have thoughts, emotions or behaviors that are out of control, especially when they are affecting your relationships, your work or your sense of well-being, never feel embarrassed to ask for help. Especially at times when you are upset, depressed or in despair.

When you are struggling to deal with personal life challenges, remember that your issues may be your own but could also be effecting the lives of others you care about.

When the use of alcohol or drugs interferes with your health, your emotions, your relationships, your job or your ability to fulfill your daily responsibilities, this is also a sign that you need help outside of yourself.

When you are confused, distraught with emotions, and need the perspectives of a caring yet unbiased person to help sort among difficult choices, do not be afraid to reach out to someone you trust for help.

Lastly, when you feel that life is no longer worth living, that you are hopeless and have reached the end of your rope, and your last option is that you would rather die than keep living with the pain of the present. In the midst of this kind of distress and despair, you are not prepared to make any life or death decisions. Talk to someone you trust. Ask for help!

God cares for you so much that He has prepared and placed people around you to help you deal with your issues. You are not alone. You are not the only one. There are others who have been through exactly what you have been through and made it out victoriously, just so they can help you.

They are waiting on you.

I'm waiting on you.

God is waiting on you.

You are the reason why God impressed it upon me to write this book. Just for you.

He knew that you would be reading this book, right now, as you are silently struggling in private to overcome a battle that you were never meant to fight alone. Trust Gods sovereignty. Don't let the quiet devil keep you silently trapped inside of your circumstances when God has provided you a way of escape to victory.

TERRY D. SWAIN

ABOUT THE AUTHOR

TERRY D. SWAIN is the author of both *3D Ministry – Maximizing Your Ministry Potential* and *The Quiet Devil*. He is a native of Alabama, who currently resides in Georgia, with his wife and two children. He is an influencer, thought leader, philanthropist, mentor, speaker and entrepreneur, who empowers people, families, communities, organizations and businesses to succeed. He is co-founder and host of *The Blacklight Interviews, Terry's Table* and *Real Men Real Talk* Podcasts. He is the founder of *The Swain Foundation*, a not for profit organization that is focused on partnering, volunteering, serving, and giving to help those who are underprivileged, underserved and disenfranchised.

www.terrydswain.com

TERRY D. SWAIN

TERRY D. SWAIN

Made in the USA
Columbia, SC
01 July 2019